Monthly Planner
2016

Copyright © 2014

All rights reserved. No part of this publication may be reproduced, distributed or transmitted in any form or by any means, including photocopying, recording, or other electronic or mechanical methods, without the prior written permission of the publisher, except in the case of brief quotations embodied in critical reviews and certain other noncommercial uses permitted by copyright law. For permission requests, write to the publisher, addressed "Attention: Permissions Coordinator," at the address below.

Speedy Publishing LLC
40 E. Main St., #1156,
Newark, DE 19711
www.speedypublishing.co

Publisher's Note: This is a work of fiction. Names, characters, places, and incidents are a product of the author's imagination. Locales and public names are sometimes used for atmospheric purposes. Any resemblance to actual people, living or dead, or to businesses, companies, events, institutions, or locales is completely coincidental.

Speedy Publishing LLC©2014

Ordering Information:
Quantity sales. Special discounts are available on quantity purchases by corporations, associations, and others. For details, contact the "Special Sales Department" at the address above.

Monthly Planner 2016 -- 1st ed.
ISBN 978-1-6328794-9-3

JANUARY

S	M	T	W	T	F	S
					1	2
3	4	5	6	7	8	9
10	11	12	13	14	15	16
17	18	19	20	21	22	23
24/31	25	26	27	28	29	30

1 friday

2 saturday

3 sunday

4 monday

5 tuesday

6 wednesday

7 thursday

8 friday

9 saturday

10 sunday

11 monday

12 tuesday

13 wednesday

14 thursday

15 friday

16 saturday

17 sunday

18 monday

19 tuesday

20 wednesday

21 thursday

22 friday

23 saturday

24 sunday

25 monday

29 friday

26 tuesday

30 saturday

27 wednesday

31 sunday

27 thursday

FEBRUARY

S	M	T	W	T	F	S
	1	2	3	4	5	6
7	8	9	10	11	12	13
14	15	16	17	18	19	20
21	22	23	24	25	26	27
28	29					

1 monday

____

____

____

2 tuesday

____

____

____

3 wednesday

____

____

____

4 thursday

5 friday

6 saturday

7 sunday

8 monday

9 tuesday

10 wednesday

11 thursday

15 monday

12 friday

16 tuesday

13 saturday

17 wednesday

14 sunday

18 thursday

19 friday

20 saturday

21 sunday

22 monday

23 tuesday

24 wednesday

25 thursday

26 friday

27 saturday

28 sunday

29 monday

MARCH

S	M	T	W	T	F	S
		1	2	3	4	5
6	7	8	9	10	11	12
13	14	15	16	17	18	19
20	21	22	23	24	25	26
27	28	29	30	31		

1 tuesday

2 wednesday

3 thursday

4 friday

5 saturday

6 sunday

7 monday

8 tuesday

9 wednesday

10 thursday

11 friday

12 saturday

13 sunday

14 monday

15 tuesday

16 wednesday

17 thursday

18 friday

19 saturday

20 sunday

21 monday

22 tuesday

23 wednesday

24 thursday

25 friday

29 tuesday

26 saturday

30 wednesday

27 sunday

31 thursday

28 monday

APRIL

S	M	T	W	T	F	S
					1	2
3	4	5	6	7	8	9
10	11	12	13	14	15	16
17	18	19	20	21	22	23
24	25	26	27	28	29	30

1 friday

2 saturday

3 sunday

4 monday

5 tuesday

6 wednesday

7 thursday

8 friday

9 saturday

10 sunday

11 monday

12 tuesday

13 wednesday

14 thursday

15 friday

16 saturday

17 sunday

18 monday

19 tuesday

20 wednesday

21 thursday

22 friday

23 saturday

24 sunday

25 monday

26 tuesday

27 wednesday

28 thursday

29 friday

30 saturday

MAY

S	M	T	W	T	F	S
1	2	3	4	5	6	7
8	9	10	11	12	13	14
15	16	17	18	19	20	21
22	23	24	25	26	27	28
29	30	31				

1 sunday

2 monday

3 tuesday

4 wednesday

5 thursday

6 friday

7 saturday

8 sunday

9 monday

10 tuesday

11 wednesday

15 sunday

12 thursday

16 monday

13 friday

17 tuesday

14 saturday

18 wednesday

19 thursday

20 friday

21 saturday

22 sunday

23 monday

24 tuesday

25 wednesday

26 thursday

27 friday

28 saturday

29 sunday

30 monday

31 tuesday

JUNE

S	M	T	W	T	F	S
			1	2	3	4
5	6	7	8	9	10	11
12	13	14	15	16	17	18
19	20	21	22	23	24	25
26	27	28	29	30		

1 wednesday

2 thursday

3 friday

4 saturday

5 sunday

6 monday

7 tuesday

8 wednesday

9 thursday

10 friday

11 saturday

12 sunday

13 monday

14 tuesday

15 wednesday

16 thursday

17 friday

18 saturday

22 wednesday

19 sunday

23 thursday

20 monday

24 friday

21 tuesday

25 saturday

26 sunday

27 monday

28 tuesday

29 wednesday

30 thursday

JULY

S	M	T	W	T	F	S
					1	2
3	4	5	6	7	8	9
10	11	12	13	14	15	16
17	18	19	20	21	22	23
24/31	25	26	27	28	29	30

1 friday

2 saturday

3 sunday

4 monday

5 tuesday

6 wednesday

7 thursday

8 friday

9 saturday

10 sunday

11 monday

12 tuesday

13 wednesday

14 thursday

15 friday

16 saturday

17 sunday

18 monday

19 tuesday

20 wednesday

21 thursday

22 friday

23 saturday

24 sunday

25 monday

26 tuesday

27 wednesday

28 thursday

29 friday

30 saturday

31 sunday

AUGUST

S	M	T	W	T	F	S
	1	2	3	4	5	6
7	8	9	10	11	12	13
14	15	16	17	18	19	20
21	22	23	24	25	26	27
28	29	30	31			

1 monday

2 tuesday

3 wednesday

4 thursday

5 friday

6 saturday

7 sunday

8 monday

9 tuesday

10 wednesday

11 thursday

15 monday

12 friday

16 tuesday

13 saturday

17 wednesday

14 sunday

18 thursday

22 monday

19 friday

23 tuesday

20 saturday

24 wednesday

21 sunday

25 thursday

29 monday

26 friday

30 tuesday

27 saturday

31 wednesday

28 sunday

SEPTEMBER

S	M	T	W	T	F	S
				1	2	3
4	5	6	7	8	9	10
11	12	13	14	15	16	17
18	19	20	21	22	23	24
25	26	27	28	29	30	

1 thursday

2 friday

3 saturday

4 sunday

5 monday

6 tuesday

7 wednesday

8 thursday

9 friday

10 saturday

11 sunday

12 monday

13 tuesday

14 wednesday

15 thursday

16 friday

17 saturday

18 sunday

19 monday

20 tuesday

21 wednesday

22 thursday

23 friday

24 saturday

25 sunday

26 monday

27 tuesday

28 wednesday

29 thursday

30 friday

OCTOBER

S	M	T	W	T	F	S
						1
2	3	4	5	6	7	8
9	10	11	12	13	14	15
16	17	18	19	20	21	22
23/30	24/31	25	26	27	28	29

1 saturday

2 sunday

3 monday

4 tuesday

5 wednesday

6 thursday

7 friday

8 saturday

9 sunday

10 monday

11 tuesday

12 wednesday

13 thursday

14 friday

15 saturday

16 sunday

17 monday

18 tuesday

22 saturday

19 wednesday

23 sunday

20 thursday

24 monday

21 friday

25 tuesday

29 saturday

26 wednesday

30 sunday

27 thursday

31 monday

27 friday

NOVEMBER

S	M	T	W	T	F	S
		1	2	3	4	5
6	7	8	9	10	11	12
13	14	15	16	17	18	19
20	21	22	23	24	25	26
27	28	29	30			

1 tuesday

2 wednesday

3 thursday

4 friday

5 saturday

6 sunday

7 monday

8 tuesday

9 wednesday

10 thursday

11 friday

12 saturday

13 sunday

14 monday

15 tuesday

16 wednesday

17 thursday

18 friday

19 saturday

20 sunday

21 monday

22 tuesday

23 wednesday

24 thursday

25 friday

26 saturday

27 sunday

28 monday

29 tuesday

30 wednesday

DECEMBER

S	M	T	W	T	F	S
				1	2	3
4	5	6	7	8	9	10
11	12	13	14	15	16	17
18	19	20	21	22	23	24
25	26	27	28	29	30	31

1 thursday

2 friday

3 saturday

4 sunday

8 thursday

5 monday

9 friday

6 tuesday

10 saturday

7 wednesday

11 sunday

15 thursday

12 monday

16 friday

13 tuesday

17 saturday

14 wednesday

18 sunday

19 monday

20 tuesday

21 wednesday

22 thursday

23 friday

24 saturday

25 sunday

26 monday

27 tuesday

28 wednesday

29 thursday

30 friday

31 saturday

www.ingramcontent.com/pod-product-compliance
Lightning Source LLC
Chambersburg PA
CBHW080042260726
48658CB00007B/2702